In Quietness & Confidence

Life Lessons, Small Revelations and Whispers from God

By

Nichole Taylor Compton

Best Man Entertainment
Louisville, Kentucky

In Quietness & Confidence

Life Lessons, Small Revelations and Whispers from God

Nichole T. Compton, J.D., M.B.A.

In Quietness and Confidence:
Life Lessons, Small Revelations and Whispers from God

Copyright © 2013
Nichole Taylor Compton

ALL RIGHTS RESERVED
No portion of this publication may be reproduced, stored in any electronic system, or transmitted in any form or by any means, electronic, mechanical, photocopy, recording, or otherwise, without written permission from the author. Brief quotations may be used in literary reviews.

Unless otherwise indicated, all biblical scriptural quotations are taken from the New King James or original King James Version of the Bible.

ISBN-10: 0991148118
ISBN-13: 978-0-9911481-1-0

For information, contact:
Nichole Compton
P.O. Box 34641
Louisville, KY 40232
motivation@NicholeCompton.com

Please visit her website for more info, inspirational insights and other product offerings, or to book her for speaking:
NicholeCompton.com.
Online ordering is available for all products.

Cover photo of Nichole Compton taken by Ty Lockhart Photography

Printed in the U.S.A.

In Memoriam:

Mae Hobbs, George Hobbs, Wood Taylor III,
Ethel Mae Chavis Taylor, Betty Taylor
and
Jamila R. Harris Grant

Contents

	Prologue
	Testimony
1	My Favorite Part of the Book of Job
2	Nowhere But Up
3	My "Job Moment"
4	Master Plans
5	Faith and Physics
6	When It Rains…
7	Action Required
8	It's ALL Good!!
9	Eagles
10	Sunshine Above the Storm
11	Trust Your Gut
12	Never Forget
13	Success is Best Revenge and Redemption
14	Ram on the Other Side
15	What Did You Just Say?
16	"Take Me" Days and "Make Me" Days
17	Lord Grant Me the Serenity
18	Mind Your Own Business
19	Busting Out
20	Don't Stop Before the Finish Line
21	Today Is the Special Occasion
22	Forging Your Own Path (The Road Less Traveled)
23	Seeing Life in Color
24	Happiness Is a Decision
25	Patience
26	A Laughing Matter

Contents (continued)

27 Anything Worth Doing Is Worth Doing Well
28 Decisions, Decisions
29 Don't Be the Fool
30 Live In The Present…
31 "Dear John" Letter to the Past
32 Simple, But Profound, Statement
33 Moment Of Temporary Insanity
34 Refocus
35 In the Moment
36 A Case of the "Surelys"
37 Beauty for Ashes
38 Meant for My Bad, Used for My Good
39 Lesson of the Day
40 In a Blink of an Eye
41 Mansion and a Yacht
42 Confessions
43 Lights Out
44 Write It Plainly. Proclaim It Boldly
45 The Best Worst Ever
46 Can't Nobody Do You Like You
47 Only Need One Yes (Maybe Two)
48 Joy in the Morning
49 Rumble, Baby, Rumble!!
50 Life Is Good
51 Fake It 'Til You Make It
52 Final Thought
    Dedication
    About the Author

Prologue

In the best years and even the toughest times in my life, I have almost always kept a prayer journal. As I prayed, dreamed, and read, I documented my "ah-hah" moments and revelations. Years later I am coming out of a valley experience and rocketing to glorious victory through no one other than Jesus Christ himself.

My belief has always been that we go through our valleys in life, what I call our "Job moments," and hard times to be able to bless others. There is always some lesson in everyone's life that can be shared to prevent someone else from going through heartache or a testimony that is exactly what the doctor ordered to give someone else a good case of what I call the "Surelys" (surely if God can do it for you, He can bless me too).

This Book is intended to share the tidbits that I picked up over time, tidbits of wisdom that came as "ah-hah" moments and small whispers of the angels who God has placed in my life for the moment.

The book is not a novel or a perfect literary treatise, but it was simple and written from the heart. It can be read cover to cover at once or just opened when you are in the need or encouragement or a sobering word of advice.

My beautiful God-fearing mom constantly reminds me that "no man is an island." So I pray my this book enriches your daily life and blessed you in every situation.

Peace and Blessings.
~With sincerity, love, quietness and confidence

Nichole

My Testimony

Believe it or not these two pages were the hardest part of writing this book set.

The saying goes "You can't have a testimony unless you have been tested." My testimony includes so much in my short life thus far and is one that is still in the making...tests included. However, I firmly believe God is not finished with me yet...or my testimony. To Him, be the glory.

I have been encouraged to include my testimony by loved ones aware I was writing books and told that I HAD to share to possibly encourage others.

So here goes the short version:

I survived and you can too. Looking back over the years, I see how I was kept and how even in my worst hours God was at work making things work for my good. I have been through watching my best friend pass away before my eyes after years of battling breast cancer as a young woman; being a teen mom and fighting not to be a negative statistic as so often easily happens and is predicted; surviving a tumultuous divorce and affair which brought ridicule, heartache and caused major losses unexplainable; deception; losing my dream home that I built; my car catching fire; starting up and closing down businesses; bankruptcy; foreclosure; unexpected job layoff (before even starting the position...imagine that); losing friends and making new; backstabbing; gossip; public defeat after losing a county-wide election; surviving car wrecks (not my fault) including being hit by a city bus; hair falling out and bald spots; betrayal; more failures; barrenness when wanting a child only to have my husband's mistress giving birth to not one but two illegitimate children during my marriage; my child hospitalized long term for years on end; single parenthood; bouts with self-doubt and unwarranted self-esteem lows; loved ones with mental illnesses and the related issues; being the one to discover my grandmother paralyzed on the floor after her stroke; surviving shingles as a 29 year old (which is almost unheard of) and other near death experiences in the hospital a few times; lupus; near death asthma attacks; law school; three educational degrees; being on welfare; heartbreak; lonely nights; theft and the list rolls on.

I am definitely not proud to say I have experienced most of the above, but I am proud to say I survived. That is just the tip of the iceberg and a glimpse of my 34 years of life. Some experiences are still too fresh to comprehend and some are just too hurtful to dredge back up right now. *(Besides, if you want the rest, you will have to read my other books.)*

But I share all of that to say this: I have been through that and much more ….<u>and yet</u> I still stand.

Don't get me wrong! Oh, I have my "days" and everybody does, but that is where this journal comes in. Use it as a tool to still be encouraged and stay determined to still move forward. Get quiet, reflect, write, cry, laugh and regain and retain your strength. I hope this book richly blesses you.

IN QUIETNESS AND CONFIDENCE, I SHALL REGAIN AND RETAIN MY STRENGTH

*THIS IS WHAT THE SOVEREIGN LORD, THE
HOLY ONE OF ISRAEL, SAYS: "ONLY IN
RETURNING TO ME AND RESTING IN ME
WILL YOU BE SAVED.*
**IN QUIETNESS AND CONFIDENCE IS
YOUR STRENGTH…"**
ISAIAH 30:15 NLT

1 My Favorite Part of The Book Of Job

Job 38-41 New Living Translation (NLT)

The Lord Challenges Job

38 Then the Lord answered Job from the whirlwind:

² "Who is this that questions my wisdom
   with such ignorant words?
³ Brace yourself like a man,
   because I have some questions for you,
   and you must answer them.

⁴ "Where were you when I laid the foundations of the earth?
   Tell me, if you know so much.
⁵ Who determined its dimensions
   and stretched out the surveying line?
⁶ What supports its foundations,
   and who laid its cornerstone
⁷ as the morning stars sang together
   and all the angels shouted for joy?

⁸ "Who kept the sea inside its boundaries
   as it burst from the womb,
⁹ and as I clothed it with clouds
   and wrapped it in thick darkness?
¹⁰ For I locked it behind barred gates,
   limiting its shores.

¹¹ I said, 'This far and no farther will you come.
   Here your proud waves must stop!'

¹² "Have you ever commanded the morning to appear
   and caused the dawn to rise in the east?
¹³ Have you made daylight spread to the ends of the earth,
   to bring an end to the night's wickedness?
¹⁴ As the light approaches,
   the earth takes shape like clay pressed beneath a seal;
   it is robed in brilliant colors.
¹⁵ The light disturbs the wicked
   and stops the arm that is raised in violence.

¹⁶ "Have you explored the springs from which the seas come?
   Have you explored their depths?
¹⁷ Do you know where the gates of death are located?
   Have you seen the gates of utter gloom?
¹⁸ Do you realize the extent of the earth?
   Tell me about it if you know!

¹⁹ "Where does light come from,
   and where does darkness go?
²⁰ Can you take each to its home?
   Do you know how to get there?
²¹ But of course you know all this!
For you were born before it was all created,
   and you are so very experienced!

²² "Have you visited the storehouses of the snow
  or seen the storehouses of hail?
²³ (I have reserved them as weapons for the time of trouble,
  for the day of battle and war.)
²⁴ Where is the path to the source of light?
  Where is the home of the east wind?

²⁵ "Who created a channel for the torrents of rain?
  Who laid out the path for the lightning?
²⁶ Who makes the rain fall on barren land,
  in a desert where no one lives?
²⁷ Who sends rain to satisfy the parched ground
  and make the tender grass spring up?

²⁸ "Does the rain have a father?
  Who gives birth to the dew?
²⁹ Who is the mother of the ice?
  Who gives birth to the frost from the heavens?
³⁰ For the water turns to ice as hard as rock,
  and the surface of the water freezes.

³¹ "Can you direct the movement of the stars—
  binding the cluster of the Pleiades
  or loosening the cords of Orion?
³² Can you direct the sequence of the seasons
  or guide the Bear with her cubs across the heavens?
³³ Do you know the laws of the universe?
  Can you use them to regulate the earth?

³⁴ "Can you shout to the clouds
  and make it rain?

³⁵ Can you make lightning appear
   and cause it to strike as you direct?
³⁶ Who gives intuition to the heart
   and instinct to the mind?
³⁷ Who is wise enough to count all the clouds?
   Who can tilt the water jars of heaven
³⁸ when the parched ground is dry
   and the soil has hardened into clods?

³⁹ "Can you stalk prey for a lioness
   and satisfy the young lions' appetites
⁴⁰ as they lie in their dens
   or crouch in the thicket?
⁴¹ Who provides food for the ravens
   when their young cry out to God
   and wander about in hunger?

The Lord's Challenge Continues

39 "Do you know when the wild goats give birth?
   Have you watched as deer are born in the wild?
² Do you know how many months they carry their young?
   Are you aware of the time of their delivery?
³ They crouch down to give birth to their young
   and deliver their offspring.
⁴ Their young grow up in the open fields,
   then leave home and never return.

⁵ "Who gives the wild donkey its freedom?
   Who untied its ropes?
⁶ I have placed it in the wilderness;
   its home is the wasteland.

⁷ It hates the noise of the city
   and has no driver to shout at it.
⁸ The mountains are its pastureland,
   where it searches for every blade of grass.

⁹ "Will the wild ox consent to being tamed?
   Will it spend the night in your stall?
¹⁰ Can you hitch a wild ox to a plow?
   Will it plow a field for you?
¹¹ Given its strength, can you trust it?
   Can you leave and trust the ox to do your work?
¹² Can you rely on it to bring home your grain
   and deliver it to your threshing floor?

¹³ "The ostrich flaps her wings grandly,
   but they are no match for the feathers of the stork.
¹⁴ She lays her eggs on top of the earth,
   letting them be warmed in the dust.
¹⁵ She doesn't worry that a foot might crush them
   or a wild animal might destroy them.
¹⁶ She is harsh toward her young,
   as if they were not her own.
   She doesn't care if they die.
¹⁷ For God has deprived her of wisdom.
   He has given her no understanding.
¹⁸ But whenever she jumps up to run,
   she passes the swiftest horse with its rider.

¹⁹ "Have you given the horse its strength
   or clothed its neck with a flowing mane?
²⁰ Did you give it the ability to leap like a locust?
   Its majestic snorting is terrifying!

²¹ *It paws the earth and rejoices in its strength*
when it charges out to battle.
²² *It laughs at fear and is unafraid.*
It does not run from the sword.
²³ *The arrows rattle against it,*
and the spear and javelin flash.
²⁴ *It paws the ground fiercely*
and rushes forward into battle when the ram's horn blows.
²⁵ *It snorts at the sound of the horn.*
It senses the battle in the distance.
It quivers at the captain's commands and the noise of battle.

²⁶ *"Is it your wisdom that makes the hawk soar*
and spread its wings toward the south?
²⁷ *Is it at your command that the eagle rises*
to the heights to make its nest?
²⁸ *It lives on the cliffs,*
making its home on a distant, rocky crag.
²⁹ *From there it hunts its prey,*
keeping watch with piercing eyes.
³⁰ *Its young gulp down blood.*
Where there's a carcass, there you'll find it."

40 *Then the* L*ORD* *said to Job,*

² *"Do you still want to argue with the Almighty?*
You are God's critic, but do you have the answers?"

Job Responds to the L*ORD*

³ Then Job replied to the LORD,

⁴ "I am nothing—how could I ever find the answers?
   I will cover my mouth with my hand.
⁵ I have said too much already.
   I have nothing more to say."

The LORD's Challenge Continues

[verses omitted here]

41
¹¹ Who has given me anything that I need to pay back?
   Everything under heaven is mine....

I know that the above excerpt from the book of Job is long, and for some of us, is more scripture reading than we have done in a *LONG* while. I decided to include it all because it always made me remember something simple: God is great and God is good. He is great, meaning, He is able to do all the things as mentioned in the passage. And He is good, because He loves us and is good to us.

2   Nowhere But Up

The beauty of hitting whatever you consider rock bottom to be is that there is nowhere to go but up. For some, the thought of having to get back up is overwhelming or that person may just be comfortable lying around in the pits for a little while. But eventually you have to get up and make some kind of move.

Rock bottom is not such a bad place to be. From there, there is nowhere to go but up. Get up! Look up! Rise up!

3 My "Job Moment"

I think everyone at some point of their life feels like they have experienced a "Job moment." For those who don't know, Job was a faithful servant who loved God and did all he knew to live right. He was a good father and husband, etc. Satan saw that Job was favored by God to prosper and be in good health.

Being the hater that satan is, He was in conversation with God and basically told God Job only served Him because He had a hedge of protection around him and treated Job well. God said "Not so!" and allowed satan to test Job as long as he didn't kill Job. That's when satan had a field day! Job begin losing everything: kids, friends, health, wealth, possessions, everything. Everything?

EVERYTHING! ... or so it seemed.

Job was faithful despite what his friends and neighbors tried to convince him of. He was consistent and adamant to the end that he trusted God; however, towards the end of the story (right before the excerpt I included begins), Job quietly questioned God.

About 5 years ago, I experience what I marked as my "Job moment." A defining moment in my life where it seemed as if someone had entered my living room and exploded a stick of dynamite powerful enough to blow up and destroy my world as I knew it! It all started with the revelation that my husband had been having an affair, and despite the fact that I had tried to get pregnant for four years, the mistress was pregnant. After that, I began to lose everything. My health worsened, my happiness seemed to be a distant memory, and I went from being a stoic strong woman to crying uncontrollably. My son became suicidal and starting acting out. My business went quickly suffered as I could not concentrate on anyone's problems, especially when it seemed I couldn't handle my own. My finances then suffered.

Before long, things has gotten so bad so quickly, that I joked one day that I was having my "Job moment," pointing out that the only thing I didn't have was the painful open sores he had. A few days later I came down with a bad case of shingles (…and at the age of 29!!!!) That was almost unheard of by my doctor and I was 36 years too young to qualify for the vaccine for it. Me and my big mouth! I later learned not to joke, but at least Job got to keep his spouse. I was left to suffer through my moment alone. [That was not all that occurred. The calamities and headache and heartache spanned a few more years past that and included much more than I could ever list here. That is another book I am writing altogether.]

Well, since I had claimed I was having a "Job moment," I forced myself to actually read <u>all</u> of the Bible's account of Job, which was somewhat of a daunting task, but I did it... and boy was I glad I did. When I got to the excerpt I included above this entry, I couldn't stop reading. For me, it quickly put things back in prospective. God is just. God is great. God is good.

I don't want to serve a wimpy God. After reading this, I realized I didn't. So if you skipped it, I recommend going back and really taking in what it says, for it puts things nicely in prospective.

As for the story of Job, God blessed him and restored to him what he had lost. Matter of fact, he recovered a double portion of everything he had lost. God blessed the latter part of his life more than his past. I only pray that my "Job moment" results in double for my trouble too.

4   Master Plans

> *"For I know the plans I have for you," says the LORD. "They are plans for good and not for disaster, to give you a future and a hope."*
> Jeremiah 29:11 New Living Translation

He doesn't always reveal what the Master Plan entails. Instead, He gives us instructions and lets us peek at the plan in doses. But like He never changes, neither does His Plan. It is always good and to see you prosper.

5   Faith And Physics

Balls that slam to the ground bounce a higher distance than they traveled downwardly.

Physics is an interesting subject to me. It contains both the law of inertia and gravity. And being an attorney, I like law, because theoretically, a law is constant and consistent in the outcome.

Gravity, simplified, naturally pulls objects down towards the earth, including humans, which is why we don't float away into space. The law of inertia causes items to continue doing what they are doing unless acted up in by some type of force. So in other words, objects at rest stay at rest unless acted upon by a stronger force.

So let's take a ball, for instance.

If you drop a rubber ball, it bounces.

If it accidentally falls, it bounces.

If you slam it to the ground, it bounces!

It may roll forward, but only after it bounces at least once. The harder the ball hits the ground, the higher the resulting bounce is.

My sister once pointed out to me, after I had gone through yet another tough moment in life, that if I was the ball, I was destined to rocket sky high. At that time, I had just been slammed to the ground with what seemed like an immense force. Had I not known better, I would have sworn I splattered, leaving remnants of the happy, strong, confident me everywhere. Instead, she pointed out that if I used the force that had thrust me downward positively, then I naturally should be soaring upward on an awesome rebound. Up, up and away! I was stronger with greater potential and learned lessons from the way down.

The lesson in this is: use the moment of the downward thrust, along with any lessons you learned on the way down, to take you to astronomical heights. You are only broken or splattered if you choose so. The better choice is to bounce back!

6 When It Rains…

I was blessed to spend my 21st birthday living in Accra, Ghana, in West Africa. I was there for a few months living with a surrogate family. Many Americans have a misconception of how West Africa really is.

The city of Accra is the capital of Ghana, West Africa and is a hidden paradise. Palm trees line the streets and the city sits on the ocean's coast with breath-taking views of crystal blue waters and miles of sunshine. The <u>entire</u> time from the moment I arrived, the days were nothing but sunshine and not a cloud in the sky. I found an ocean-side café next to a 5-star hotel. The café had an outdoor terrace that overlooked the ocean with a dance floor, swanky tables with tropical umbrellas, and live music like something out of a romantic movie. My plan was for my friends and me to celebrate my 21st birthday and dance the night away to the vivacious live band while eating exotic food into the wee hours of the morning.

Well, nature had another plan. You see June is also the tropical "rainy" season for that part of the world. And while the weather had been quite deceptive the weeks prior, on my birthday, the heavens opened up and the rain poured down. The rain was so heavy that you could not see your hand in front of your face. So I spent my birthday looking out of the window and wishing for the rain to seize. It never happened. So much for the party I had envisioned.

But one thing that I remember every Ghanaian, including my surrogate mother, saying is that I was so very blessed that a downpour happened on my day. They believe that rain signifies blessings. Without rain, nothing grows and without growth (and crops) there is no prosperity. So in their culture, the rain meant I would be blessed and prosperous in the upcoming year. And while I wanted to cry as hard as the rain was pouring down, they were all rejoicing for me in what was to come.

I felt stupid afterwards and ended up making the most of what I felt was a bad day, because I realized something I have kept dear to me to date:

IT IS ALL ABOUT PROSPECTIVE.

It's important for me to keep a positive one no matter what. Matter of fact, I try not to dread the rain anymore. Now every chance I get I rejoice in, run in, walk in, twirl in, skip in and dance in the rain. I like the thought of growth, blessings and prosperity.

7 ACTION REQUIRED

Philippians 4:13 (NKJV) reads, ***"I can do all things through Christ who strengthens me."***

The scripture "I can do all things through Christ who strengthens me" is frequently quoted. But one day as I was reciting scriptures to myself, attempting to encourage myself, a revelation I never considered came to me. "Do" is an verb requiring action. This means, yes I can do all things through Christ who strengthens me, but it requires me to "DO" something. I must take action.

So many times, I have debated with friends who say that it is God's job to do everything for his children. While I do believe that He will supply all my needs and in my endeavors He will strengthen me, I also have to do my part and make sincere efforts.

Just like with my son. I have an 18 year old. Although he is now an adult and is now responsible for himself, I still love my son and want to see him do well. So when he is trying sincerely to stay on course, do well and be successful, I am going to always have his back and give him whatever he needs to succeed and support his positive endeavors. The Bible speaks of how much more Our Heavenly Father loves us and knows how to treat us better than we as earthly parents.

So, "DO" your part.

8 It's All Good!!

> ***"All things are working for the good of those who love the Lord and are called according to His purpose."***
> Romans 8:28

As a reminder to myself, I constantly used to proclaim the colloquialism *"It's ALL good!"*

When I go to the store for an item that I find is out of stock, my response?

"It's all good!"

The traffic on the expressway is backed up?

"It's all good!"

"Mom, someone just got fingerprints on the window in the living room."

"It's all good."

In all actuality, my bad news was more like this: Bank account is overdrawn because the store debited the account twice accidentally. The house may be going into foreclosure. The disgruntled worker you fired is going to your competition trying to ruin your good reputation with falsities. Your engine and transmission blew at the exact same time and you are stranded on the side of the road.

Either way, I had to remind myself, realize and acknowledge that *IT IS ALL GOOD!!!*

God had me, and as long as I was His, loved Him and continued to follow His purpose for me, things may not have seemed so, but were actually working for my benefit. Not just the good, but the bad were working in my favor too. So many times we cannot see or even fathom His plans for us or how He can use the bad for our good, but He does.

So when the engine and transmission blow simultaneously, look for the new car. At least keep positive in the face of adversity and disappointment, because, big or small, God may just be using that instance as a defining moment to show you that He is still working it all for your good!!! Repeat the three words to yourself and smile or write them when you doodle,

"IT'S ALL GOOD!"

9 Eagles

The U.S. national bird is the America Bald Eagle, in all its majestic strength and beauty. But the Bible also makes frequent references to eagles in its scriptures. Consequently, I have always been fascinated by eagles. Every chance I get, I want to learn more about them and how they live, as well as the scriptural references.

Keeping with that, I was once told during a tough time in my life, "Eagles soar alone or with only other eagles." I had never heard this expression before. I was in awe, but I was also prompted to make some defining life choices.

What I learned is that when you are attempting to soar to new heights or greatness, not everybody will be joining you for the ride. They simply cannot. The higher up you go, the bigger the risk and the harder the journey. When I think of an eagle, I think of strength, agility, wisdom, vision, integrity, fidelity (once mated, they stay committed until death) and restrained power. Not everyone has these qualities or care to acquire them. When you look at other birds, each has its function, purpose and unique characteristics. While none is better than the other, eagles have the privilege of soaring extremely high, and I imagine figuratively the closest to God. Eagles have the ability soar above the clouds and fly well during stormy weather. Coupled with their excellent eyesight, their view is spectacular and from that high up, problems must seem small, insignificant and manageable, because they are being viewed in the proper perspective, close to God.

Everyone cannot go where you go. So intend to reach greatness as an eagle, and desire the qualities and privileges of one, you must remember, you may just be soaring alone. Be sure to get close to God and aim high.

10 Sunshine Above The Storm

Recently, I was flying to visit a friend. The weather reported a terrible storm was to occur between the airport and my destination. As we boarded the airplane, I could see the rain starting. And as the plane took off, we experienced a good amount of turbulence. In fact, I am a frequent flyer and avid traveler, and that was the greatest amount of turbulence I had experienced.

Once the airplane ascended and settled above the clouds, I took notice of something amazing that I knew but was so relevant in that moment. The sun was shining. I peered intently out the window next me taking note and in awe of the whole scene. As we coasted above the storm, I could see the clouds and see the lightening occurring in the clouds. But I also could see the sun shining above the clouds and unaffected by the storm below. There was a calm and peace about the sky as we cruised above the storm and the rain. Those on the ground for certain could only see the rain as it fell to earth. That, however, did not mean the sun did not exist. In fact, it did. It was shining beautifully and continued to the whole time.

Wow! What a lesson this became for me. Now I know that in those moments when it seems like life is pouring down on me, God is still shining and at work. And although it seems like everything is dark and cloudy in life, the sun is still shining, and other forces are still at work beyond what I can see, feel, or sense.

11 Trust Your Gut

Whether you believe in the Holy Spirit or not, most people at least believe in a gut feeling. My belief is that we all have "gut feelings." Further, if we have them, they must be there for a reason.

I know personally, when I have second guessed that "gut feeling," I have almost always regretted it later.

When you are true to yourself and that nagging inkling you get in the midst of making a decision, you cannot go wrong. Trusting your gut means trusting yourself and your God given sense.

> **GUT =**
>
> **G**od-given wisdom
>
> **U**
>
> **T**ake everywhere

12 Never Forget

NEVER, NEVER, NEVER FORGET:

1) Whose you are,

2) Who He is!!

3) What He promised

and

1) What He already has done.

[<u>Hint:</u> Start with #4. Start writing and recalling what He's already done and what blessings you are thankful for and the rest will be easy.]

13 Success is The Best Revenge

And Redemption

I have always been defiant or stubborn, rambunctious and determined to succeed. Whenever I have been told that I cannot do something, I strive to not only achieve the feat but do it bigger and better than what I was told I was not able to.

When rejected or underestimated, I have always told myself that success is the answer. Aiming for traditional revenge is not worth the energy or time. The best revenge and/or redemption is success. Use the negative energy, feelings, and emotions to positively fuel and motivate you towards greatness. Push every limit that your opposition, the world, and naysayers put on you. You can push their limits with your achievements until the limits inevitably recede.

So when you are hurt or you feel defeated, rejected, or underestimated, pick a task or goal that you would like to accomplish and give it all you have. Give it your "all." Use it to better yourself. Give it all your energy, focus, and free time. Use the negative energy and emotions for positive gain, regardless if anyone else notices or pays attention.

You define your limits. Actually, God does (and with Him nothing is impossible) but it requires you to act and believe. Finally one day you will look up and the goal will be well-done and you will have distracted yourself from negative thoughts or emotions. Success will be your revenge and/or redemption. And you better believe the world cannot help but to take notice.

(Regardless, by then you won't care. Just be proud of yourself and happy in your own success and accomplishment.)

14 Ram on The Other Side

In the Bible is the story of Abraham and the ram in the bush. I used to gloss over this story and only read it when I needed to remember how Abraham had unwavering trust in God and faith that God was just and would provide. I always desire the same trust and faith he possessed.

But about a year ago, while studying my Bible, I had a revelation that has made that story one of my favorites in the Bible.

In case you do not know the story, I will paraphrase. Essentially, God told Abraham to take his son Isaac (the same son God promised Abraham and Sarah in their extremely old age, his miracle child) and sacrifice him. Abraham did as instructed and took his two servants and some donkeys, his son and some wood, and went to the mountain He left his servants at the foot of the mountain and took the wood and his boy up the mountain to the site where he was going to sacrifice. His son asks along the way where they were going and you know he had to be calculating in his mind "I see the wood and stuff to start a fire and stuff to slaughter the animal, but …..um….what is dad going to sacrifice. All that is left is me."

Abraham did not know what God planned but figured if God told him to sacrifice either He would provide, but if it came down to it and he was supposed to sacrifice the miracle child God gave Him, then God must have a reason and Abraham was obedient. Right as Abraham strapped his son Isaac down and was about to sacrifice his son, God stopped him and showed Abraham a ram caught in the thicket of a nearby bush. This was to be used to sacrifice and that was God's plan all along. He was pleased with the trust, faith, and obedience that Abraham showed.

Now the reason I grew to love this story is this. The story is told from Abraham (and partially Isaac's prospective) usually; but what about the ram? No one ever considers the ram's journey. His part of the story is that brief moment when Abraham notices him and Isaac's life is spared. However, the ram is an important piece to this story. The ram had a destiny, mission, and purpose. God was in control all along and for each step Abraham and Isaac made up the mountain, so did the ram.

God's timing and preparation was and is perfect, as well as His forethought. While we don't know and can't see what is taking place on the other side of our mountain,

God is all-knowing and all-seeing. He has already provided for us; so our task is to keep taking the steps, keep moving higher and higher up the mountain, and know that God has a reason, a plan, and your solution is already on its way.

15 What Did You Just Say?

Be careful what you speak. I believe that God created us in His image. His Words are powerful and even caused the world to be formed. So if we are in His image, what we speak over ourselves, our situations, and our dreams and desires, have power. If for no other reason, the things we meditate and speak on can change how we feel about ourselves and situations.

16 Take "Me" Days...
and Make "Me" Days

Take "Me" Days.

...Make "Me" Days.

When my best friend Jamila was alive, she would schedule us what we called "me" days. They usually consisted of going to the thrift store to browse, stopping at McDonald's for a big cup of sweet tea with lemon, or going to get our nails done or a massage. Sometimes we would go to a restaurant we had been eying or just stay over one or the other's house to watch a movie and do each other's hair.

Most "me" days were simple and did not cost much but were days to do something simple that made us happy and smile and sit back and appreciate the simple things in life. Jot down a few things you may want to do for a "me" day. Be sure to refer to the list and start treating yourself and making time to make a "Me" day.

Celebrate being you. Yay, You!!

17 Lord Grant Me The Serenity

Serenity Prayer

*God grant me the serenity
to accept the things I cannot change;
courage to change the things I can;
and wisdom to know the difference.*

*Living one day at a time;
enjoying one moment at a time;
accepting hardships as the pathway to peace;
taking, as He did, this sinful world
as it is, not as I would have it;
trusting that He will make all things right
if I surrender to His Will;
that I may be reasonably happy in this life
and supremely happy with Him
forever in the next.
Amen.*
                    ~ Unknown Author

There is a great debate over where this prayer originated. Many years back, it was adopted by 12-step recovery program, used to help people change their lives around and recover from addictions and negative habits. I never realized, until recently, how powerful this short prayer was, or that it was more than just the first four lines, but it has helped me in recovering from my negative habits (albeit not drug or alcohol related).

I am naturally a control freak. I am the eldest sibling of eight. Secondly, I have been a mother since age 16. And I am naturally an "A-type" personality. This characteristic has been a blessing and asset to me in some instants, such as running my own law firm and managing others. However, being controlling and wanting to control everything is not always productive or healthy in other aspects and areas in life.

Sooooooo, I had to physically post this in my bathroom for a period of time and recite it to myself. This was to help me realize many things, but most importantly that what I can control, I should and that I should not be afraid to do so if I can. And those things that I cannot control will not end my world. That I have to surrender the desire to get overwhelmed, frustrated or sad and know it will be ok.

Since, I have learned (and am still learning) to roll with the punches and live one day at a time, sifting through what challenges I control, and taking on one issue at a time.

Posting the full prayer and reciting it often worked for me. Consider doing the same and intently digesting the meaning of each line.

18 Mind Your Own Business

I believe that there is an order to everything, and everything should have its own place and function.

However, clamoring to solve the problems of my son, my mate, my family members, and others close to me, I had once become overwhelmed. I was at wit's end and beginning to be frazzled. Every decision I made was based on and much of my stress stemmed from <u>things that I could not control</u>…until one day a friend, Nicole, said something so profound, yet elementary.

I worried how to make things better for others and how to make things work to make them more comfortable for others or lessen the blow of consequences of others that naturally stemmed from their ill-decisions. She pointed out that three types of issues exist in the universe. I am only responsible for one. There are issues that are God's business, e.g. the sun rising, the weather for the day, gravity, etc. There is other people's business, e.g. the consequences of their decision, what they wear, what they eat, if they get a job or vacation, etc. My business is simply to tend to me and carry out my God-given purpose.

While this is not the exact message she imparted that day, the gist is the same. Once I actually considered what she was trying to say, a heavy burden was listed. I have since used this as a measure before concerning myself with any issue. This way I mind my own business (and that has proven to be just the measure I can handle anyway).

19 Busting Out

***Just when the caterpillar thought its world was over,
it became a butterfly.***

Recently, I saw a picture of a guy busting out of an earth. The picture wasn't the best but the message was profound. It said something to the effect that in an egg, live is cultivated. If an outside force breaks the shell, the life inside ends prematurely but if the shell is broken from the force on the inside, life begins.

The same holds true for the caterpillar. The beauty produced is only seen <u>after</u> the struggle. If a caterpillar is manually peeled out of its cocoon, it is weak and vulnerable, dying almost immediately. But if allowed to emerge on its own, a beautiful creature is birthed with strength to spread its unique, colorful wings and fly. And while the butterfly displays magnificent colors and designs, all it knows is that it has survived what seemed to be a near death experience and the struggle of its lifetime.

Matter of fact, the butterfly cannot see its new colors, except I imagine in the reflection of piece of glass or a crystal clear water source. I presume that one day it notices that awe-struck expressions on the faces of other creatures mesmerized by the obvious transformation. The butterfly even after discovering its wings, most likely does not even realize the magnitude of its transformation as much as those viewing from the outside. I would assume that even neighboring insects and animals that saw the caterpillar disappear for the while that it did, assumed that the caterpillar was dead and gone.

Not so. The butterfly is definitely a testament to the scripture "my latter shall be greater than my past." Remember, when it seems like you are being overtaken, nearly defeated and close to the end, the end of the world as you know it, may be the beginning of a beautiful life in which you are transformed into someone awe-inspiring and with newfound strength. Watch God work, and the facial expressions and the jaws drop around you as others see just what awesome person you have become.

20 Don't Stop Before The Finish Line

Imagine your task is to run a race, the length of which is unbeknownst to you. All you know is that the undetermined length is not more than you can bear. So although you don't know how long you have to go, you are not restricted in how long you manage to complete it either. You can run, walk, skip, crawl, scoot, or whatever. Now lastly, the other catch is that you have to run the race eyes closed or blindfolded. You know that the direction you are moving in is correct but the rest is left to faith and trust of those coaching and coaxing you to complete.

At times, you can hear their cheers and encouragement loud and clear, but sometimes it seems like your cheerleaders are far away and you have to keep encouraging yourself, "Just one more step." "Keep going self." "You can do this." Your only instruction is to keep going straight ahead, and you will know when you have reached the finish line, because you will be able to feel it, after which, you will be able to look back and see the accomplishment you made.

So the task at hand and the race is made just according to your skill set and strength and no more, which means you just may to have to muster and use everything you have in you to complete the race.

Now let's also imagine you just can't take anymore at some point. The race seems like it's taken forever, you have scooted, crawled, ran, walked, dragged yourself and even prayed your way a little. Regardless, you just can't go any further.

Your coach, the cheerleader, or race official asks repeatedly "Are you sure?" Giving it much through, you decide for the prize (which may be unknown) and the risk of having to keep going perpetually, you just can't or better yet, it is just not worth it to you. And you quit. You give up and crash to the ground in exhaustion, not caring to muster any more second winds. You then rip the blindfold from your face, peel open your eyes and adjust your vision to the sunlight before you...only to realize that you were there. You landed and lay one hair's length from the finish line. You were so close that if the finish line ribbon were a snake, you would have been its next meal for certain.

Now imagine that feeling, the feeling of unnecessary defeat and giving up before receiving the prize when you were oh so close. You work so hard to hold on and for God to bless you with what you desired and prayed so fervently for … but you give up a tad too soon. OUCH!!

This was the visual I repeated in my mind over and over to help me survive years of tests and trials. And each moment when I hurt so bad, and was so exhausted thinking I just couldn't go another stretch believing and having faith that better days were ahead or that I would ever see what I prayed for, the thought of being "right there" and giving up seconds too soon, was always enough to give me a second wind, another ounce of fight and renewed determination.

So the next time, you are considering and thinking of throwing in the towel on whatever race or task you are attempting to finish or achieve, close your eyes and visualize the above scenario.

21 TODAY IS THE SPECIAL OCCASION

Today is a gift that is why it's called the present.

Yesterday is gone.

Five seconds ago is already the past.

Tomorrow is the future, and even the next moment is not promised, so all you have is NOW.

So TODAY is the special occasion you are saving that special occasion outfit for, the day to use the good silverware you only pull out every once in a while in that special house guest comes to visit.

(pssst… Here is a secret you are the most important guest in your home. Use the china and the silverware today…JUST BECAUSE.)

What are you saving the best for?

Today is the special occasion; the day to wear that special dress is today. CARPE DIEM[*].

([*]Translation: Seize the Day)

22 Forging Your Own Path

Although you may be traveling seemingly with the same goal or in the same direction as others, your path, experiences, and potentials are unique to you. Not only should you not be distracted by your past, but who's doing what around you really doesn't matter either.

Stop looking back, looking around, or getting down (and discouraged).

2) Get on your mark (figure what you are trying to do);

3) get set (set your goal), and only look up (to God for direction and strength);
and

4) go forward taking the next step he places before you.

Always keep moving, one foot in front of the other in your own world and in your own lane.

...And run 'til you're finished.

The Robert Frost Poem "The Road Not Taken" is one of my favorite poems. I had to memorize it as an 8th grade Language Arts class assignment. Since then, I recite the poem quite often. Matter of fact, when I travel and speak to groups nationally, I always require the audience, however big or small, young or old, to close their eyes as I read it to visualize and feel the words. But the best line to me, the line that says it all, is the last. It sums up how I have chosen to live my life. (It has not always been grand, but has always had its own rewards and definitely been something to write about.)

"Two roads diverged in a wood, and I...I took the one less traveled by and that has made all the difference."
~ Robert Frost

23 Seeing Life In Color

I have always been a rigid "type-A" personality. I even joke that my blood type is A+ (It really is.), but in my world everything is "cut and dry," black and white, either or, and no in-betweens. I realized, the hard way of course, that there are more options than black and white sometimes. And you can live in the gray spots. Things may not always make perfect seem or be so simple or "cut and dry."

So I started looking for the gray areas. And while I admit they were scary, because not so predefined, it was also liberating. That was until I was scolded by a friend for being so closed-minded, (who me? I gasped. Naw! Not me.) while living in the gray. "Why do you focus on living in the black and white and grays? See life in color, full color. The reds, the blues, the greens, the browns, wonderful pastels, et cetera." She said, "There are never just two solutions to a problem. You have a universe filled with many options."

So now I may start with the black and white, and then dabble in the grey, but I constantly have to remind myself that the world is in color and so we should live.

Look for the colors. There lies a pretty rainbow of infinite beautiful colors if you just open yourself up to see the vivid possibilities.

24 Happiness Is A Decision

A friend of mine repeatedly told me "Nikki, your happiness should be paramount to everything." I realize that statement is not an absolute always, but was relevant to me at the time. It was exactly what I needed to hear. Essentially what he meant was that I have to keep focused on what makes me happy, to the extent that I have control over it.

I have to consciously choose opportunities to be happy. This may mean disappointing others or saying no, but that may just be necessary. Once I got this concept, I realized that it was ok not to do what others wanted me to do or not to overextend myself for something that was not going to add to my happiness or even have a negative effect on me.

I also had to realize that in the midst of situations that were uncomfortable for me, I had the choice to be happy. I could either let the circumstances get me down and flustered, or I could choose to be happy in the midst of the bad situation. I learned that choosing to be happy made the situation more bearable.

No one else is responsible for my happiness but me. This applies to you also. You are responsible for making and keeping you happy. Not your spouse, not your friends, not your mate, not your kids, not your parents. Sometimes you have to consciously make the decision to be happy. Others can only share in or enhance the level of happiness you already create for yourself and own. So make yourself happy. Happiness is a decision…and an important one at that.

25 PATIENCE

One of my actual personal journal Entries from 12/09/08:

This morning I finally acted on an old bright idea of mine to text daily scriptures to loved ones. Well the scripture I randomly picked up and texted was ***"Count it all joy when ye fall into diverse temptations, knowing this, that the trying of your faith worketh patience." James 1:2-3.*** Later in the day I told my sister, Sheree, that I was intending to pray to God and ask for a check-up to see if I was in His will, but I was within His will but just losing patience. I still haven't asked God. Too scared and too many distractions. So I sat down at 11:30 pm, opened a new book I bought, and read the first chapter, which boldly said something that gave me a WOW revelation. Satan is not strong or able to be everywhere all at once. He is not all knowing or almighty like God, so he relies on other strengths. Satan is careful in his planning. Strategy is one of his strongest points. As children of God we need patience to beat him at his own game.

26 A Laughing Matter

Take the time to laugh. Go ahead laugh now. Laugh because the sky is blue. Laugh because of that one time your arch enemy had a booger in his nose. Laugh just to be laughing. If you can, go turn on a funny comedy show or sit and people watch for a few minutes (you are guaranteed to notice something to stir a chuckle or two). Even if you don't have the time right now, make it.

AT LEAST take the next 30 seconds and give the best heartfelt, stomach-wrenching laugh you can give. Sometimes, I find that I have to laugh to keep from crying, but it works. Laughing is a healthy distraction from negative feelings, and amazingly your body and brain physically will follow suit.

27 Anything Worth Doing is Worth Doing Well

I have for years preached to my son that you do your best at all times, even if no one will ever notice. The truth is that you don't know when someone will notice. And anything worth your time should be done to the best of your ability. After all, your reputation is on the line. And you want whenever someone speaks of you to be the best report possible.

Numerous stories have been told of someone entertaining their boss or someone powerful who could help them in other ways and not knowing it. Those encounters have led to jobs, raises, public accolades and other major blessings. But just as those stories exist, so do the ones of the lazy employee whose boss showed up unexpectedly to find the employee had haphazardly done a task or the person who did something unethical only to be caught or exposed or cause some irreparable damage.

Anything work doing is worth doing well.

28 Decisions, Decisions

Every decision you make affects more than just you. Every moment of every day, you can make a choice to change everything forever.

You are not living in a bubble. You are surrounded by family, friends, loved ones and strangers constantly. Your decisions therefore affect more than just you. Every decision has a consequence and can cause a ripple effect. Let's use drunk driving for example. You party hard and decide to try to drive home. Obviously, you are affected in that you are risking your life and taking a chance on making it home safely. Additionally, you are putting everyone on the road that you pass at risk as well as their loved ones. You take the chance of causing an accident. If you do cause an accident, now you have involved your loved ones who will be left to worry and figuratively pick up the pieces.

This was a lesson I learned at the tender age of 15. My son's father got me pregnant on purpose (Believe me, being an unwed or teen mom was never my intention). Having sex was a decision I assumed only affected me and well him. (It definitely only satisfied him. I was dumb.) But I soon learned I affected so many more. I hurt and let down my parents. I remember this being the first time I really saw my strong father cry. I watched helplessly as certain church choir members ridiculed and whispered about my mother, definitely an innocent party. I watched as my son grew up without a father in his life and an unwed mother most of his life. I negatively influenced my younger siblings and friends who assumed being a teen mom was easy from observing at me (and never did I know I made it look easy, because it sure as heck wasn't). I let down other family members and people looking up to me that I didn't even realize. Finances were affected and much more.

Since then, I have raised my son to know that any and all of his decision affect more than just him and that every moment of every day, a choice to change everything forever can be made. Our choices change everything forever, like my choice to have premarital sex that one instance changed my life's forever. So while you may have made a bad decision or a decision with bad consequences, you can attempt to correct it by deciding to make different future choices.

Choose wisely, if not for your sake, for those around you.

29 Don't Be The Fool

Fools learn from repetition and experience; the wise learn from watching the fools.

Fool learns the hard way. The wise learn from fools. From the time I was young until now, all of my friends, family members I hung with and even boyfriends were much older than me. I learned at a young, young age that it seemed much better to see what others did wrong and learn from their mistakes instead of having to go through the hard times myself to figure it out.

Fools learn from repetition and experience; the wise learn from watching the fools.
In other words, fools learn the hard way and the wise learn from their mistakes.

30 Live in the Present and Live Realizing Every Moment is a Present

Yesterday is the past. Tomorrow is the not promised. That is why we call today the present. Live *in the present* and live realizing that *every moment is a present*. Unwrap life, as each breath is gift.

31 Dear John Letter To The Past

I loved the Disney movie *The Lion King* when I was a kid. My favorite part of the movie is when the wise baboon elder hit the young lion on the head and taunted, "It doesn't matter. It's in the past."

However comical to watch, that has been a lesson that to date I struggle with constantly. I get stuck or stagnant in my progress looking back over past events with regret or wondering, analyzing and re-analyzing what could have been, should have been, was supposed to had been but didn't work out, wasn't or really would have been horrible if it had been. We are supposed to learn from our past and remember the wisdom gained but it is not wise to be petrified wasting time dwelling on it.

I frequently write in a journal to refocus, regroup and unload mental baggage. So one day, I had to write a quasi-poem/Dear John letter to my past. I will say that I do not profess to be a poet, but have decided to share the piece for the meaning. I hope it moves you to consider letting go with being stuck in the past if that is your issue and moving on towards all the wonderful potential your future holds.

Dear Past,

I wish you the best. Farewell.

Too bad I can't stay. Sorry. I am leaving you for another...my Future.

Now is the moment for me to realize that what was in the Past is just that....my Past. My heart longs for the unknown and the possibility that my new love brings and how the lovely the Future will be; but as for you and me, I can't continue to dwell with you or on you and wish things were how they used to be. So I am moving on, moving forward, moving forward without you, yet rest assured, I will never ever forget you.

Oh and by the way you can have everything we had together, but my lessons earned and my dreams, 'cuz some things are better left behind with you, too heavy to carry with me and meant to be only an old memory. So yes my estranged love and fair-weather friend, I must go and have to leave you. So long, farewell, good ridden and goodbye. Sorry for such a bitter sweet end.

My new love is much more attractive, bigger and more sincere. Cloaked in hope and dealing prosperity. Future says life is what I make it and I see the possibilities with my Future are endless. Not sure how long the newest of this love affair will last but I plan to continue 'til it's finished.

32 Simple, But Profound, Statement

I cheated on my fears, broke up with my doubts, got engaged to my faith, and now I'm marrying my dreams.

This is a simple saying that came to me and I wrote in my journal. I think it is self-explanatory and worth sharing.

33 Moment of Temporary Insanity

MOMENT OF TEMPORARY INSANITY: …now back to the regularly scheduled program…sorry, almost slipped.

You are allowed to have an "off" moment, i.e. a moment of temporary insanity (Keyword: TEMPORARY). It is not desired but sometimes it is inevitable. Cry, scream, yell, sulk, or whatever you need to do, but let it last no longer than a MOMENT. So whatever it takes to distract you from having a "moment" and keep moving in a positive direction do it.

My sister Reese taught me to laugh for 30 minutes and that instantly cures a moment of temporary insanity. I have a friend who walks and another who works out vigorously to cope. I turn positive music on and dance like no one is watching. If not able to stop and dance, I flash the biggest smile and look upwards. It works for me every time. Find what works for you. Just remember if you have a temporary moment. Quickly get back on track and they should be few and not last long!

34 REFOCUS

"FOCUS MS. COMPTON and let's get it!!!!"

The statement above is what I had to tell myself when I was so easily off track and/or starting to get sad or slow down in working towards my goals. Having it on the wall above my computer and sometimes as a screensaver tended to help. So now insert your name, read and repeat!!

FOCUS __ [insert your name here] __ and let's get it!!!!

35 IN THE MOMENT

I have naturally always gravitated toward older friends, not for their age but their wisdom. A lesson learned from my friendship with my closest friend was "Learn to just live in the moment and do you."

I am an A-type personality, and naturally focus on planning for the future and have high expectations. Just living in the moment was hard for me, but I learned soon enough that if you focus on doing just doing what made sense for the moment and enjoyed living every moment, then I could make every moment good. And good moments eventually add up. Before you realize it, when every moment is good and one day you will realize that those moments have become a lifetime of good moments.

Life is good.

36 A Case Of The "Surelys"

I am always excited to see others around me blessed. It makes me catch what I call "a case of the Surelys," which is a disease I wish I could infect everyone with. You see, if others can get good news, be blessed, and do wonderful things, then **surely** I can too! Motivated and successful people usually travel in packs because it is hard for both traits to not be contagious.

Too many times, it is easy to look around at others being blessed or getting something nice and start feeling like "woe, is me" or "that kind of stuff never happens to me." And you know what? **It sure won't if that is your mentality**. Try instead rejoicing when those around you get blessings. If nothing else, a positive "case of the Surelys" is surely better than being down in the midst of someone else's happiness. Besides, you would want them to be happy for you, so you can fully enjoy your moment.

37 Beauty for Ashes

So when all seems to have gone up in smoke, find comfort in the promise of beauty for ashes. You do not know what can come from it.

I remember reading an article about an interview with Tavis Smiley. For those who don't know him, Tavis is a world renowned author, political commentator, and host of PBS's show *Tavis Smiley*. Well originally Tavis had a promising career and hosted a late night talk show on BET for a long while. One day that was suddenly and abruptly interrupted. His show was cancelled I believe, and he was fired, let go, or whatever you want to call it. He was no longer going to be doing what he considered his "dream job." At first, Tavis was depressed and disappointed. He felt betrayed and definitely wasn't expecting his job to end with his contract not being renewed. He couldn't figure why or what went wrong. Everything seemed to be going so well.

After a while, Tavis received the opportunity to start his own radio show and be on others' shows. This gave him more freedom, opportunities, and a wider reach. Eventually, the success of that show led to him having his own show on PBS. To the point, in the interview Tavis revealed that BET cancelling the show was such a blessing in disguise. Since then, he has been much happier and doors have opened to opportunities he would have never had have come from what seemed at the time like the death of his career, or at least a tragedy. God used that to make beauty from ashes.

For years, I carried around that tattered and torn article as reminder that with the death of one thing, new beginnings for another may be the result.

I read somewhere that "Sometimes God has to let your dream die, so that His vision for you can come alive."

We, as humans, have free will and that we are free to dream and to do and to make decisions. But it also says that He has a plan that is good and customized for each of us. After all, He fully knew us before we were.

Just as when my son reached 13, suddenly he thought that he knew exactly what was best for him. He was sure that he should be taking over from that point. However, as a parent, I knew what was best for him and what I envisioned was much better. I knew that allowing him to completely take over everything was not it!! When he allowed me to manage the details of his life, life for him was smooth and he was happy (not happy he was not the boss but happy overall) and the end result was great. The same goes for us and Our Heavenly Father.

I think I would rather have what He wants for me than to have it my way. After all, if He made me then surely he knows what makes me happy and the things I like. I trust that it would be better than I could even imagine.

38   Meant for My Bad,

Used for My Good

Hehehehehe....rotflmbo and smiling at every negative force, energy and person placed in my life that shall propel me to my full potential! ;-))

I believe that everything happens for a reason, even the bad stuff. And I firmly believe that even the bad stuff is used to make you who you are supposed to be, especially if it makes you more conscientious and you learn from it. Use everything the good the bad and the ugly as a stepping stone and positive force to get you to you reach your destiny and full potential.

Successful people are strong and smart enough to build a foundation from the bricks thrown at them.

39 LESSON OF THE DAY

Look for the good in every moment and every situation.

I had a friend (we will call her Friend A) who always expected the worse out of someone. I remember one day, a mutual friend (we will call her Friend B) did not answer or return Friend A's call. Immediately, Friend A was ready to write Friend B off, assuming that she didn't call or answer because of Friend B's bad intentions or ill-will towards Friend A.

Immediately, I stopped Friend A from proceeding down that way. I told her, "You cannot think the worse and always look for the negative plausible answer." In fact, Friend B could be in the hospital or at home handling a disaster. Believe it or not she may just have been genuinely busy or forgot.

Our human nature seems to be negative. Or maybe it is culture. But I firmly believe you should look for the good in every moment to enjoy each precious moment. And look for the good in every situation. Give people the benefit of the doubt as well. You never know. Better to have thought positively and been wrong than the embarrassment and hurt caused by vice versa.

40 IN A BLINK OF AN EYE

Life is unpredictable. That is why we must live in and enjoy every moment. I have had many friends recently experience unforeseen tragedies including deaths that seem to have come unexpectedly in the blink of an eye. So it keeps making me think.

Just as life as we know it can change that fast for what seems like the worst, it can be changed to the best just as fast.

Expect good things. We do not know what God has in store for us JUST RIGHT around the corner in life. What if you blink and with one phone call, one letter, or one event, EVERYTHING you ever wanted, dreamed or imagined happened. Your life really can change for the better instantaneously.

Remember good old Job in the Bible? Just as quickly as Job lost it all, he also recouped double but not when he preferred but instead at a moment when he least expected it.

Be a prisoner of hope. Zechariah 9:12

41 A Mansion and a Yacht

"My Name is Nichole Compton. I own a mansion and a yacht."

One day I was driving my friend and her fiancé to the port for them to catch a cruise ship. As we drove along the beautiful roads of Miami, my friend commented on how nice the boats were. I commented, "Yeah, I wish I owned one."

She quickly stopped me and reminded me of what I actually usually remind others: "Speak what you desire. Your words have power." It first starts with an idea or desire but if never spoken or expressed, that idea or thought fizzles.

I quickly rephrased what I said and blurted confidently, "My name is Nichole Compton. I own a mansion and a yacht…..and a jet!" She giggled and confirmed with a smile, saying "See there you go!"

I remember growing up there was a cartoon character, on Woody Woodpecker's show, that repeatedly introduced his self that way. "My name is ____. I own a mansion and a yacht." Then watching it as a kid was entertaining, but now I mean business. My goal really is to own a mansion, a yacht and, oh yeah, my jet. And I don't intend to stop there.

When will I get it? I don't know. I am sincerely working on it. But this I do know: I will get it. And I will continue to speak it until I see it!

Just who are you? And what do you declare?

42 Confessions

"I need to figure what I want to be and who I am. I have it written down but need to make it clear and succinct!!! Today starts day #1 for the new me. I am going to walk in my millions until it comes to past. No one has to know right now how much is or isn't in my bank accounts. I am going to proceed as if I already have my mansion and yacht until I see it."

That was am actual entry from one of my journals. The truth is that our victories start with our confessions. We have to act on it, but first, we have to be able to see and say it with our mouth. Every motivational speaker (and preacher), that I have ever heard speak on the subject, basically says the same. Your words have power. Whether you use hypnosis or repeat a mantra to help remind you, being able to verbalize your goals and dreams is a recommended positive start, even when you physically don't have it or can't see it.

As I write this book, I do not have a million in the bank, but daily I confess it, and I am not willing to waver (and if I accidentally do, it is only for a short while). It is coming, and step-by-step, I am working hard on earning my millions, getting my mansion, my yacht, and of course I can't forget, my jet.

While your goal or thing you are confessing may not be as big or daunting as it seems to be a millionaire, the same concept applies.

43 Lights Out

Everything pivots on your attitude and perception.

One of my favorite examples is from my childhood. When my siblings and I were young, my parents struggled financially at one point. I remember the electricity in our home being cut off for a night. My mom made it fun and told us we were camping. We lit candles, rolled out our blankets, played games and told stories. It turned into great family time. While I am sure my parents were worried and probably embarrassed, my savvy mother made the best of the moment. It never happened again that I remember but that memory lasted forever! We, as kids, had such a ball that we were sad we never had another camping night.

Thanks to my mom's creativity and positive attitude and thinking, a bad situation was a great memory and our perception was it was a great night, when in actuality it was really not the best situation.

Your happiness is YOUR happiness. Your attitude and perception play a big part in how happy you are. CHOOSE TO BE HAPPY.

44 Write It Plainly, Proclaim It Boldly!

Take today and write yourself your own proclamation. The one above is one of the many that I have done over the years and it got me through a lot. Add scriptures, sayings or declarations that you need to hear, ones that will add flesh to your goals and proclamation. The bible talks about writing the vision and making it plain. Take time today to think big. What is your next step in life? What is your ultimate step? What is the person you want to be?

> ***Then the LORD answered me and said, "Record the vision and inscribe it on tablets, that the one who reads it may run." For the vision is yet for the appointed time; It hastens toward the goal and it will not fail. Though it tarries, wait for it; For it will certainly come, it will not delay...."***
>
> Habakkuk 2:2-3 New American Standard Bible

45 THE BEST WORST EVER!

My son happened to be hospitalized long-term without any sight of a release date or improvement. And although it was Mother's Day, no visitation allowed that day as it wasn't a visiting day on the hospital schedule. My husband, who had left home to be with his mistress, was celebrating mother's day with her as she was either pregnant or had just had one of their children. Money was funny and nothing seemed just right. And on top of it, it was nasty and gloomy outside and pouring down rain was the weather.

Before the day came, I decided that if this was the worst Mother's Day that I had that it would be the BEST worst Mother's Day ever, and that I was going to love me and the enjoy myself in that moment. I took myself to dinner (which consisted of a Starbucks and a KFC chicken finger meal) read a book I had been wanting to read, I went to the nail shop and got a pedicure and treated myself to a movie at the dollar movie theater.

While I can't remember what book I read or what movie I watched, I distinctly remember letting a sigh of relief and satisfaction at the end of the day, because instead of being defeated, I had the best worst Mother's Day ever. And the next year, Mother's Day rolled back around, and sure enough the next Mother's Day had similar circumstances, and wasn't all I wished it could be either. But that year, I was ready -mentally and emotionally ready- to be happy and make the best in spite of the apparent circumstances. And that year beat out the year before to become the new best worst.

So when things seem bleak, or that you are in the worst situation or day of your life, make your worst, the BEST WORST EVER!!

46 Can't Nobody Do You Like You

I read a Facebook post once that read something to the effect, "I have met that perfect someone for me and I love them dearly. They think and say and do all the right things. They are always there for me and no one can do me better. I LOVE ME! So much so I wish I could marry me."

While marrying yourself is taking it a little far, the statement has validity. Before expecting someone else to, you should be able to love you first and be good to yourself. Many miss this mark.

So if you were unsure before reading this or just plainly didn't know it, I am telling you now. YOU ARE SPECIAL and YOU ARE IMPORTANT. This world does not have another you, so you must love you! Besides no one be you. Be happy in your skin, meaning be true to whom you are. No one else can emulate or imitate you and all your unique and wonderful qualities. No one can be you and do you like you. Daily, I am learning to love me. I tell everyone what you see is what you get because I only know how to be Nikki… and Nikki is perfectly imperfect.

Celebrate you and never compromise who you are.

47 Only Need One Yes (Maybe Two)

No one likes rejection. But rejection is a part of life. I remember watching a weekend marathon of the movie The Bodyguard. And while the movie was playing, they showed fun facts and little known tidbits about the movie, the actors and the script. One of the facts listed said that the movie was rejected 59 times before being accepted to be produced. But once it was produced it went straight to the top of the box office, made lots of money and produced the number one selling song "I Will Always Love You" as sung by Whitney Houston, which took the music charts by storm. One yes and the rest was history.

Similarly, in life all we need is one "Yes" (maybe two). A "Yes" from God goes a long way! It definitely goes longer than the one "Yes" from The Bodyguard's movie producer. If we are in His Will and following the path we are supposed to, that one "Yes" will pave the way for everything else we need. And just like the movie received all kinds of accolades and achievements, the same positive accomplishments will flow in our lives with that one "Yes."

The second "Yes" needed? Well, that is the one for you from you. You have to be able to see and believe in the "Yes."

Can I do this? YES

Do I have what it takes? YES

Am I willing to give this venture my all? YES

Do I have the trust and faith to get me through this? YES

Your "YES" coupled with God's "YES" is all the approvals you need. Mute the haters, ignore the naysayers, and give up trying to convince the unbelievers and sometimes even the "well-meaners." The vision you have and the mission God sends you on is sometimes, no, most times, between you and him. Others may not understand it or believe it or be able to fathom it. But their approvals, yes, no or otherwise, do not matter anyway.

48 Joy In The Morning

More times than I care to count, I remember one person or another reciting in an attempt to comfort, "Weeping may endure for a night, but joy comes in the morning." Of course, this seems like an age old cliché, but it comes from the Bible verse Psalms 30:5.

It was not until 2010, that this scripture, saying, cliché, took a new life and meaning for me.

In 2010, I ran for a District Court Judge seat in my community. For those who don't know, this was one of the biggest personal challenges and one of the most defining, life changing moments for me. And aside from that it was also one of the most devastating moments in my life. I put everything on the line to run. And when I say everything, I mean EVERYTHING. Finances, faith, health, time, reputation, my marriage, family, and more. EVERY THANG! (Not to mention, I almost definitely gained a lifelong enemy I didn't intend).

I was the youngest person on the ballot (and in hindsight the most politically naïve) attempting to unseat the judge who had been on the bench the longest. [A suicide mission some said, but I had my reasons and the past judicial polls were good enough reasons.] Many instances occurred on the campaign trail that could have caused turning points for my campaign, both positive and negative. I was determined that no matter what I would be to be true to me and my reasons for running for such a position, and to continuously maintain my integrity. I was adamant that regardless the outcome, I was giving it my best effort and would not engage in activities that were unethical or went against what I believed.

Well needless to say, I ran a good race. And considering my campaign did not raise as much money as I wished, and the circumstances of being a young, minority female and going against seemingly a Goliath without as much as a slingshot or a rock, I was fortunate in that I won about 1/3 of the total votes (with no money, few political connections and no experience running a race), but a loss was a loss and in my eyes, at that time, any loss was a miserable loss.

However, I was lucky enough to have a true friend, who at the time was my best friend and hero, Everett Morton (self-proclaimed social genius). As so many times before, he was right by my side with the right word of advice and was able to get through to me. [I can be stubborn and thick-headed sometimes and always hard on myself. (shocking, I know!) ☺]

That night Ev told me, "Nikki, I know you are hurt. You have every right to be. You worked hard and it did not turn out like you hoped. So…" he said, "I am going to allow you to cry all night. I will hold you through the night and you can cry on my shoulder. Don't get snot on me too much," he jokingly added, "but get all your tears out; because in the morning, when the sun comes up, it's a new day. You have too much to offer the world not to keep moving and continue doing the things that God has for you to do."

And I did, I cried most of the night. (I did not snot on his shoulder, but I am grateful he allowed me to cry.) Every time I thought about how embarrassed I thought I was and how I really wanted, no needed, a win, I cried more.

But sure enough, the sun rose again and morning came. And in the morning, no more tears were allowed. [As a friend and someone mentor, I respected him and his demands on me to make me be the best Nikki I could be.]

So now this is something I live by and have shared when being a friend to or mentoring others. You get one moment, whether it be five minutes, for minor stuff, or a whole night for major hurt and pain, but you only get one moment to cry.

Joy comes in the morning, especially if you make it. You have to choose to be happy. So while crying is normal and negative emotions are normal, you must set limits to them. We all have something great that we are supposed to be doing. So have your moment, but quickly get back on track and get to doing whatever that is!!

[And keep good, wise, "old" people as friends, the ones who know a little bit and love you enough to be stern, shoot straight with you and give tough love when needed. That always helps.]

49 RUMBLE, BABY, RUMBLE!!!

One day recently I found myself dwelling on everything that I have been through in my recent past. My eyes watered up and then I caught myself. "Nikki, you have to fight this. FIGHT!!" Instantly, this is what came immediately to mind and I jotted it down as I reminder. I hope this helps you too.

FIGHT!!!

F - Forget the Past. Forgive yourself. Focus on healing.

I - Initiate your plans for the future. Imitate what life you want. In other words, fake it 'til you make it.

G - Get ready. Get off your butt. And Go forward (one step at a time)

H - Hear from God. Heed His Word/Will. Head in the direction of where you want to go.

T - Take by force!! Trust and Try. (Give it your best effort) Triumph!!!

50 Life Is Good

A Nikki Commercial Break: **When overwhelmed with life....don't forget to just BE!!**

LIVE!!

When was the last time you took a walk around the block?

Or skipped?

Or stopped at the park just to swing and kick your feet as high as you can towards the sky?

Or smiled while twirling in circles until you are dizzy?

Or childishly played and laughed in the midst of a group of kids?

Or rode a bicycle around the neighborhood with your feet up in the air and off the peddles?

Or ran in the rain just because?

Or colored in a coloring book?

(Side note: My mom hates it when I say I do that, but I do have my Precious Moments coloring book and my own crayons stashed in my safe for special moments.)

I have made it a point to do all. No matter what anyone thinks or how busy life becomes, I do it!

Life is too short. Make the most of it!

You are now returned to your regularly scheduled program
(or better yet, I hope not!)

LIFE IS GOOD!

51 Fake It 'Til You Make It

Begin acting, not according to the way you feel, but according to the way you would like to feel.

Better yet, the way I feel cannot control my life. I cannot allow my emotions and the way I feel. I need to stay focused on God, His Plan and His Will, especially in the middle of the storm when the sight (which can be deceiving) of emotion malfunction from dysfunction. Need to rely on the radar control panel which is always correct (as in a plane).

52 — Final Thought

(May not be proper English, but I intended to write it as it is written and mean it just like it sounds. To preserve the essence of how I've always said it and to be true to its meaning, I have chosen to leave it. Meditate on it just how it is.)

Today is the first day of the best days of the rest of my life.

(Because I say so. Because I choose it to be so. I hope you follow suit.)

Love life and love yourself.

Dedication

I owe so many people love, and gratitude that writing this part was difficult. I dedicate this book to the following:

Bonnie and **Charles Taylor, Sr.**, the parents who raised me to believe I could do and be anything. Mama, thank you for all your days and nights of prayers and crying out to God on behalf of your children, especially me. To Daddy, for spoiling us and making me a daddy's girl. I am blessed and honored to have you as parents. (P.S. please forgive me for any slang or grammatical errors included in this book. I am working on it still. LOL)

To my sisters, the Taylor Girls: You are all special to me and each play a major role in my life in your own way. I could not imagine life without any of you in it daily. **Shannon,** we have been partners in crime since pampers (even when you tried to tell on me and mom thought it was just your imaginary friend Le-Le, not me Ne-Ne, you were tattling on. Lol). **Charese**, big up's to you. You one offended me by calling me your big little sister, but I am so blessed that you were there to listen, help with Rico and give me the chance to heal and grow back into being the big sister. **Sheree**, I honestly do not know what I would have done without your sound advice, listening ear day and night and Godly encouragement when I just thought I could not go on one step further. Not sure how it went from me praying and mentoring you to me being the one being prayed for and needing mentoring in the game of life, but I am glad it did. **Brittany**, (that is officially Dr. Brittany), my baby. I claimed you when mama had you as my own. I have to keep remembering you are a woman and a mother now....and a great one at that. Whenever I needed to know someone was there and had my back, it was you. Thank you for always being willing to help me, no matter what the hair-brained ideas were. You may be one of the youngest but you are a definite backbone to the Taylor girls. And **Jasmine**, the baby-baby. You have blossomed into a wonderful young lady. Some days just talking to you amazes me at how smart, sensitive and caring you are. God has wonderful things in store for you. Stay focused.

My son **Rico**- Although I counted down and rejoiced for the day you turned 18. You will always be my baby. You have put me through hell and made me proud all at the same time. You have great promise on your life and I am anxious to see your great destiny, son. I love you.

My brothers, **CJ** and **Justin**, two of the finest brothers with the biggest hearts who I have no doubt would do anything for me (and the family). I always just to want an older brother but I can honestly say I wouldn't trade either of you for the world (a $100 trillion...I may have to rethink…just kidding). You two have always come to my rescue and I couldn't ask for more.

My midgets and adopted midgets. **Amiyah** (Mya Baggins), **Ayanah** (Yani), **Alijah** (Boomie), **Asaiah** (ZayZay), **Tarnell** (Duece), **Angel**, **Gabrielle** (Babby), **Breanne** (Nanna Boo), **Raelynn** (The Boss Lady), **Gary** (Gerr-Bear), **Brynlee**, **Jaxton**, **Kyler**, **Myla** (Twin 1), **Aylana** (Twin 2), my **Jeremiah** (Gungham Style - Jerry), **Jackson R.**, **Journi**, **Rayneal** and **Malichi**, and **ZyAnn**. And special love to my 2 munchkins **Talise** (LuLa) and **Tony II** (White Boogie). You changed my life and Ms. Nichole will always love you so much.

Each of you is my heart and my future. I always say I am happy just to be the Best Auntie in the whole wide world. But it is only because each of you is the best. I gladly hope to be able to keep my promises of putting you each through college, buying your first cars and helping you fulfill whatever dreams you have. Think big because greatness lies in each of you. Love you.

My **Aunt Vicki** (the best auntie a girl could ever ask for), **Uncle Kevin** (extra proud of you), aunts, uncles, my adopted sister-friend **Dianna**, my cousins (especially **Tifenee**, **Sanitria** and **Mioshey**).

To my friends who loved, protected and pushed me always, namely, **Everett** (the social genius/black Larry David with the finger in the ear) with much thanks for all the hugs old man, and **Dee, Lanetta, Dawn, Ms. Alice**, and others [forgive me if I neglected to add you on this book. Charge my head, not my heart. Besides, there are already more books in the works. Maybe you will be in one of the next] and last but not least, to the great people of God in my life who always had a seat in their office and a special place for me **Dr. Rev. Kilen Gray**, woman of God **Sandy Gray** and **Dr. Michael E. Ford, Sr.**

Insightful.

Honest.

Inspirational.

A true blessing.

Nichole Taylor Compton, attorney, mother, and mediator, is native of Louisville, KY. This book and its companion journal, also entitled *In Quietness & Confidence*, are her first literary works published under her name. This adds to her list of positive contributions and accomplishments, which includes seventeen years as a national motivational speaker.

Nichole is known for her enthusiasm, smile, positive energy and honesty. She openly shares her life story and lessons learned to do what she enjoys most, educating and encouraging others.

To book Nichole Compton to speak to your group or purchase more of her products, and other products, visit her main website: www.**NicholeCompton**.com

www.ingramcontent.com/pod-product-compliance
Lightning Source LLC
Chambersburg PA
CBHW070531100426
42743CB00010B/2046